RATS GETTING CLOSE

by

Paul Birtill

Hearing Eye

Published by Hearing Eye
Box 1, 99 Torriano Avenue, London NW5 2RX

ISBN: 1 870841 78 6

This publication has been made possible with the
financial assistance of London Arts.

Printed by Catford Print Centre
Typeset by Daniel James at mondo designo
Cover illustration: paper cut © Emily Johns

Some of these poems first appeared in the
following publications:

Psychopoetica, *Rising*, and *Ape*.

CONTENTS

NECROPHOBIA

Ironically the only cure
for most people with a
fear of death is death
itself. My father was
one and died with a
stethoscope round his
neck – listening to his
last heartbeat.

KILLING TIME

It's ten-thirty in the morning
and I sit and wonder if anyone
in the world has been bitten
by a snake yet.

Now it's eleven – surely someone
must have severed an artery by now
or died in the operating theatre.

Now it's twelve and I'm late for
my psychiatrist.

THE CORLETTES

They were three blonde sisters
and I liked them all, especially
Janet, even though my friend said
she had a face like a parrot. I
found her purple hat in the street
once and brought it round to the
house – she wasn't very friendly
and when I asked her would she go
out with me immediately said no
and shut the door in my face.
I was heart-broken she was the
first girl I had fallen unsuccessfully
in love with – looking back I suppose
she didn't like my unfashionable
scruffy appearance, not to mention
my weird friends and eccentric father.
But going out with her would have
helped me enormously in those dark
days of my sister's schizophrenia and
mother's premature death. I saw her
cleaning her front door knocker when
I was last up in Liverpool. I had a
poem in the Guardian that day and
thought of going over and showing it
to her, but I don't suppose it would
have done any good, not now anyway.

DISAPPOINTING RESULT

First in Maths
second in French
best school project
        Became a peeping tom...

Captained a team
sang in the choir
butted a bully
        A peeping tom no less...

Trustworthy and smart
popular and punctual
conformed with ease
        A budding peeping tom...

Four A levels and
a university place
but no sign of a girl-friend
It's binoculars in the park
for our son
        He's a bleedin' peeping tom...

SHARED LETTER-BOX

Stealing people's mail
is fun to do
unless of course
they think it's you.

Money and chocolates
I've had them all
and none of them
addressed to Paul.

But be careful
when you play this game
in case your neighbours
do the same.

SOLITUDE

I live in my mind
  because I find
  peace of a kind
It's easy to do
when there's only you
  no kids or wife
  it's a quiet life.

TO DEFY HUMAN NATURE
JUST FOR ONE DAY

F ght it fight it
try your best to fight it
Smash it smash it
have a go at smashing it
Ignore it ignore it
see if you can ignore it
Forget it forget it
why not just forget it
and for twenty-four hours
don't be a slime bag...

BEING DEAD SUPERIOR

The living respect the dead
for they've done it – been
through it – suffered and
arrived, safe and sound.

RATS GETTING CLOSE

Candle-lit dinners, phoney chat
compliments and kisses
who needs that?

False sentiments, unreal affection
futile gestures cheap concern
Stuff your Valentine cards
Mustn't get attached to human trash.

In sickness and in health
my fuckin' arse
expect no sympathy if your
circumstances change
plenty more shit in the sea.

Snogging in parks sharing a bath
slowies, the flicks, fucking in
a friend's flat
I'd rather be a cockroach
than a lover.

Those who make contracts
are rewarded with brats,
mortgages H.P. debts
responsibility and misery.

I'd rather have a blackout
than an infatuation
lose a leg than have an affair
Sooner be a hermit than a couple.

EDINBURGH

If it wasn't for the cars
on the streets you wouldn't
know what century you were in.
As it is I keep thinking I'm
going to be shot by a musket,
challenged to a duel or waylaid
by footpads.

IS HE STRONG?

Funny the things you think
about on a first date – like
losing a fight at school –
failing one's exams – obscure
fears and phobias. Why is it
women bring out these feelings
in us? Is it because they're so
mercenary or so obsessed with
the continuation of the species?
Strength – strength – strength
she whispered in my ear – oh dear...

UNPLEASANT COMPANY

I had to ask him to stop
calling round in the end.
He kept treading in dog-dirt
and rubbing it into my carpet.
Once he brought a friend round
and he had stood in some too.
They both sat there smiling –
the living-room stank for days.

SWEET DREAMS

My dreams remind me of
how I saw things as a
young child – everything
a bit weird and strange –
new places, new people,
odd things happening –
but wonderful too.
My dreams remind me of
the never ending adventure
of childhood.

DEATH SENTENCE

This morning at about 10.30 my doctor
told me I had six months to live.
The man who had reassured me for so
long about everything from a lump on
the arm to a pain in the chest finally
told me I was going to die.
He acted no differently from when I'd
seen him on past visits – indeed he
might have been prescribing antibiotics
for some minor virus. I wasn't even sure
if he would mention it in passing to his
wife that evening – how he'd told a young
man of thirty-six he'd be dead by spring.
When I left his surgery I was surprised
to see everything was normal outside.
The world hadn't stopped to mourn my
predicament there was no minute's silence
observed, everyone carrying on as if
nothing had happened and I felt for the
first time in my life truly isolated
truly alone – absolutely bloody terrified.
I felt like shouting for help, screaming
about the doctor and the terrible things
he'd said to me. I wanted him arrested,
shot, strung up from a lamppost, nobody
talks to me like that. I thought of
waiting for him with a br ck, but got
drunk in a bar instead…

PUBLIC HOUSES

Most boozers
are horrible places
full of losers
getting out of their faces.

Lounging on stools
letting the day slip by
talking with fools
whose only wish is to die.

They're a kind of home
albeit sad
for those all alone
and a little bit mad.

UNLIKELY POET

I told my sister I stuffed
a piece of fillet steak down
my trousers in the supermarket.
She said I bet Wordsworth wouldn't
have done that.

FOR YOUR THROAT'S SAKE
SMOKE CRAVEN A

I wish I could have been
a smoker before 1952 when
all the health scares started.
All that wonderful advertising –
doctors offering you one in the
surgery – smoking in cinemas on
buses and trains. No quitlines,
nicotine patches or warnings on
packets. No guilt worry or social
exclusion and costing much less too.
I wish I could have been a smoker
before 1952.

REPRESSED

He was so distressed when
he realised he was homosexual
he went to his local A and E.
An attractive nurse gave him
an injection of valium – he
tried to have a wank about her
when he got home.

BIG FRAUD

Have you noticed
middle-class women (often
wearing those ghastly red
ribbons) buying *The Big Issue*.
How they patronise the filthy
vendors and stroke their smelly
dogs – easing their wanky
consciences until the next
dire issue arrives...

NIGHTS

In memory of Philip Larkin

What are nights for?
nights are where we sleep
they come, time and time
over. They are to be happy
in. Where can we sleep but
nights?

Ah, solving that question
brings the dentist and the
milkman in their underpants
running down the street.

POSITIVE DISCRIMINATION

There's a little restaurant
in Chiswick where there's a
ban on courting couples and
the waiters are in wheelchairs;
the food is very good.

THE LONELINESS OF THE
LONG DISTANCE DRINKER

The drunk always stays
till the end – and leaves
with no money or memory
friends or dignity and
if he isn't barred will
not return anyway...

CANON KIRON

I was terrified of him,
though he didn't know
me from Adam, despite
announcing the death
of my mother at morning
assembly with a huge grin
on his face, and adding
snide remarks to my school
reports...

STRANGE

Where have all the
suicides gone?
why are they carrying on?
five thousand a year is
not enough so what is
going on?

Where have all the
suicides gone?
why are they hanging on?
five thousand a year is
a paltry sum just what
is going on?...

HAMPSTEAD HEATH

He was pushing sixty
obviously bonkers
asked me if I wanted
a game of conkers.

For a list of Hearing Eye
publications, please write
enclosing an SAE to:

Hearing Eye,
Box 1,
99 Torriano Avenue,
London
NW5 2RX

Alternatively, visit the Hearing
Eye website at:

http://www.torriano.org

My thanks to all the members of West Lothian Writers, past and present, whose knowledge and enthusiasm have helped me so much over the years and to Mary and my lovely family who have put up with me for a very long time.
Also a big thank you to John Wilkinson for the lovely cover artwork.

Artwork by WILKIE: johngarth.wilkinson@hotmail.co.uk